3-30-2017

To Joan ~

Under The Shadow of Your Wings

A Devotional Book of Poetry

May you sense the presence
and love of God - as you read of
His many wonders and promises ~

A R L A R . J E N S E N

WESTBOW
PRESS®
A DIVISION OF THOMAS NELSON
& ZONDERVAN

WestBow Press books may be ordered through booksellers or by contacting:

WestBow Press
A Division of Thomas Nelson & Zondervan
1663 Liberty Drive
Bloomington, IN 47403
www.westbowpress.com
1 (866) 928-1240

Interior images by Katey Sandy.

ISBN: 978-1-5127-1689-4 (sc)
ISBN: 978-1-5127-1688-7 (e)

Library of Congress Control Number: 2015917325

Print information available on the last page.

WestBow Press rev. date: 10/23/2015

Be still and know that I am God
Psalm 46:10

Dedicated to Buz, my family, and my dear Christian friends
in WA, NJ, CA and NV, and my pastor and church family
at East Woods Presbyterian Church in Vancouver, WA

"Faith is seeing the Light
when the eyes only see darkness"

Contents

Preface

Many of these poems in this Devotional, were inspired by moments that were spent on what I call my "Spiritual Sanctuary" deck, built a few years ago on the back of my house in Vancouver, WA. It is a covered deck, that overlooks a large back yard, from which many of God's wonders are visible, with a view of several majestic trees, visiting birds, and flowers and plants. As it faces West, I am treated to spectacular sunsets, as well. On this deck, I feel the presence of God so strongly, and feel He is using me as His instrument to share, through my gift of writing, about Him and how He is working in my life, and the lives of others. I try and capture the beauty and wonder of God's world, and show the joy and deep meaning to my faith.

Acknowledgements

I wish to thank my fellow poet friend, Craig E. Burgess, for his support and encouragement, and for introducing me to many poetic adventures with the Audubon Poets group in Audubon, NJ.

In addition, I am deeply grateful to my pastor, The Rev. Bill Sperry, for all his assistance, and kind encouragement in helping to make this devotional poetry book a reality.

Also thanks to Administrative Assistant, Susanne Freeman, at East Woods Presbyterian Church, for her help.

A very special thanks, and appreciation to my church artist friend, Katey Sandy, for her contribution of images of her beautiful paintings that accompany some of the poems in my book.

Introduction

This book of faith filled thoughts and meditations may be read as a weekly devotional, or for moments of prayer and meditation, to listen to God or reflect on His presence and promises, in your busy life. Take a few minutes, rest in His presence, and, as it says in Scripture, "Be Still and Know That I Am God".

I
God's Presence and Promises

Sacred Dawn

He will cover you with His pinions,
and under His wings you will find refuge,
His faithfulness is a shield and buckler.
Psalm 91:4

Under The Shadow of Your Wings

You shelter us from the storms of life,
under your wings we find comfort and peace
and refuge from our constant strife...
When we are afraid to try and fly
you encourage us to find release
with your guidance and wisdom, Lord, where we
can ride the currents of sadness and grief.

Under the shadow of your wings
we can find safety from all harm,
you cover us with your heavenly care
and walk with us in our deep despair.
You give us the strength to withstand
what life brings our way, and to help understand
that we can run, and not be weary,
and we can walk and not fall faint.

Under the shadow of your wings,
we will rise, and find hope and strength,
as we soar to new heights, and then find our rest,
near the soft, loving heart of God.

Sacred Dawn

A velvet blanket of darkness
envelops the earth with silence.
Glistening stars hold fast,
un-yielding against an indigo sky.
In the stillness, the soul is quiet, unhurried...
Distantly, a tiny glimmer patiently awaits
to welcome the soon to be daylight.
Against the ever-brightening sky,
streaks of rose-golden arrows pierce the heavens,
followed by paint-brushed ribbons
of amethyst and lapis.
As the sun ascends into the morning sky,
it is time for meditation, and prayer,
and a praise thank you O God, for your gift
of another day to give you glory,
to savor your infinite wonders,
to celebrate our faith, our trust,
our strength in you.
May we treasure this time, as we embrace
the sacred dawn of this new day.

My Spiritual Sanctuary

Wonders of God surround me, glistening in the sunlight.
Graceful leafy guardians stretch into the air, reaching heavenward,
I see them from my seat in my Spiritual Sanctuary.
Peaceful, quiet joy flows from the refreshing breezes I feel.
One of God's feathered creatures dips his head into a birdbath
savoring the cool refreshing liquid.
Touches of lavender beckon from colorful sprays of long, delicate blooms,
visited now and then by adoring, wandering wings of gold and black.
Oh, such peaceful, spiritual moments when I know God is near.
I close my eyes and breathe in His presence, and feel in my spirit
"Be still, and know that I am God"…

Prayer

Prayer is truth, and as we pray,
we open our hearts and minds to God.
We feel prayers deeper, our hearts grow bigger,
as we are connected to Him and to others.
Prayer is honesty with God,
it enlarges our perspective
and brings divine energy to our lives,
and us closer to one another.
What we think, how we feel,
what we say, God knows it all.
May our lives be a prayer,
and may we be more open to His creation,
and His heavenly guidance.
Praying changes things,
but Prayer changes us.

Embrace The Joy

Embrace the joy of our Lord
as He gives you His Mercy
and Goodness and Grace.
Embrace His Word of Forgiveness.
Look to Him for His Spirit
and Strength.
Embrace the Love from His heart
that brings Hope and Meaning
and Life…
Joy…Forgiveness…Love…
Embrace these blessings,
they will give you peace in your heart,
and draw you closer to God.

Through the Eye of Faith

Through the eye of Faith,
we see God's Majesty, His Mystery,
as our wondrous Creator.
Suspended through time and space,
the reflection of our lives is seen
in a world of love and hate…
Joy and sadness…
Honor and disgrace…
We seek forgiveness and mercy
as we struggle to find our way
and reconcile our hearts and minds
with the love of our Savior, Jesus,
as we see through the eye of Faith.

Faces of Faith

Our faith has faces that come and go,
when we are joyful, and when we are low.
Our Lord goes before us when we ask,
and gives us the strength for every task.
Jesus is our guide for the path we take,
He forgives us our sins, and every mistake.
His Goodness and Mercy are with us each day
as we reach out to Him and follow His way.
He surrounds us with love, and caring too,
He knows your pain, and listens to you.
His heart is open as you pray,
and seek His wisdom everyday…
Faces of faith are reflected in you,
as you walk with God and His love so true.

He is Always Near

God meets us in our brokenness,
and walks with us each day,
He's there to catch us when we stumble
along life's rocky way.
His Grace surrounds us with His love,
and brings comfort and strength, too,
He's there to hear our heartfelt prayers,
though our words may seem so few.
When we are troubled or confused,
He guides and helps us understand,
that we are not facing things alone,
we have hold of His Mighty helping hand,
of love and Grace and Favor,
that He gives to us each day,
so we need to thank and praise Him,
when in our hearts we pray.
We know our Faith will sustain us,
when the road seems all uphill,
Faith is not believing that God can,
It is knowing that He Will
be there for us, when life tears our world apart,
we can rely on God's amazing Grace,
and His forever loving heart.

Brokenness

Streams of life,
Dark clouds surround us,
Fearful thoughts invade the mind.
Shattered dreams,
Scattered hopes,
Feelings of loss,
Broken pieces now remain.
My Spirit lives within you;
Do not be afraid.
Reaching out,
Restoring hope.
There is healing and redemption
as we trust in Him.
Thankfully we pray with humility,
and find togetherness,
as the clouds depart.

II

The Body of Christ

Faith is Like a Pearl

For just as the body is one and has many members, and all the members of the body, though many, are one body, so it is with Christ. For in the one Spirit we were all baptized into one body-Jews or Greeks, slaves or free-and we were all made to drink of one Spirit.
1 Cor. 12:12-13

Faith is Like A Pearl

Faith is like a pearl,
strung on the necklace of our world,
by the Mighty Jeweler, Jesus.
As the strand grows longer,
we can see His Spirit shining
and encircling our hearts and lives.

Faith is like a pearl,
a precious symbol of His love,
that brings us closer to Him.
With our prayers and humility,
we can feel His Spirit guiding
our hearts and lives in harmony.

So, as an Oyster, struggles with its burden,
and receives strength from the sea,
with our Faith we receive
His Mercy and Love,
and a Blessing for Eternity.

The Face of God

The face of God is Jesus,
who surrounds me with His love.
He gives me His Grace and Mercy,
and I praise His glory above.
His Spirit lives within me,
and guides me through each day,
I walk His pathway of life and hope,
and try and follow His Way.
I seek His face when I am lonely,
and ask for hope when there is fear,
I knock on the door to receive His Mercy,
and reassurance that He is near.
Ask of Him, and it shall be given,
seek His face, and you shall find,
knock and the door will open
to His heart, so gentle and kind.
The face of God is Jesus.

The Heart of God

With His love and compassion,
God reaches out to us
to bless us with His Mercy and Grace,
bring us joy, and hope for a new day,
a new beginning.
He mends our brokenness
with His healing touch,
and gives us strength
to stand strong against the storm.
His heart speaks to us
with wisdom and understanding,
as He lifts us up, and listens to our cries
when we struggle with our burdens.
He forgives us when we do wrong
and searches for us when we are lost
to give us the peace in our hearts
we are longing for, that only is found
in the heart of God.

My Heart Is The Home of Christ

My Heart is the home of Christ,
and every beat brings the love of Jesus
into my breath...my being...
He lives within my heart, and I feel His presence
all knowing and all seeing...
I surrender my life to Him,
as I go through each day,
He might meet me in the hallway,
or at the top of the stair.
He sees and hears me,
and I know He is always there
with His abiding love and care.
He understands and loves me,
and knows the floor plan of my heart,
He always provides what I need,
with His Grace and Forgiveness,
so I can follow His Holy lead.
My heart is the home of Christ,
and in whatever room I happen to be,
I know that He will reside in me,
until Eternity.

The Heart of Worship

In the Heart of worship,
we receive the Goodness of the Lord.
He shows us our weaknesses
and our confusion within.
We discover who He is,
as He heals our brokenness,
and helps us understand our sin.
In the Heart of Worship,
we see God's loyalty,
as He reveals things to us we need
and that bring truth and honesty.

The Heart of Worship,
brings us closer to each other,
and we draw closer to Him.
We worship in truth and in spirit,
as we let His light shine through;
even when we turn away,
He leads us to the Heart of Worship,
which conquers life and spirit,
and shows us His forgiveness,
and Everlasting Love.

Look With the Eyes of Your Heart

What you are looking for, you will find
if you look with the eyes of your heart.
You will see the awe and wonder
of the Master Creator,
of Spiritual and Physical...
Darkness to light...
Water to land...Stars to sky...
Encircling Humanity...Seasons...Life...
all that is needed.
If you look with the eyes of your heart,
you will see...the reality of God, as it is... here and now...
Christ is the hope of glory...
He rises a star in your heart.
He is forever The Son of God,
Spiritual wonder-God with us.
Embrace the Kingdom of God,
create...look for the joy...
What you are looking for, you will find,
if you look with the eyes of your heart.

The Door of Your Heart

The Lord is knocking at the door of your heart,
and He is waiting...
wanting to bring you joy, peace and love...
He waits for you to give Him entrance,
and welcome Him into your life.
You have only to open the door
and invite Him in, to be surrounded
with His compassion, and caring love,
Joy and peace, receive forgiveness and Mercy,
and have His amazing Grace and Eternal Life.
The Lord is knocking at the door of your heart,
and He is waiting...
Will you open the door?

Walk In The Ways of His Heart

Walk in the ways of His heart, and the sight of your eyes.
Follow the ways of God's love, and what you see and feel
with the presence of Jesus, is His light shining around you
as you step closer to Him...
Walk in the ways of His love, and the forgiveness of hearts
that have been wounded...
Follow the ways of His healing, and your life will be renewed.
He will take your brokenness and make you whole again,
He will bring you closer to Him, and surround you with Peace.
As you trust and believe, you will walk in the ways of His heart,
and His healing love, forever.

In The Hands of God

In the hands of God, I find my refuge,
in the hands of God, I can find my way,
He knows my weakness and my strength
and leads me through each precious day.
I lift up my hands to reach to Him,
He touches them with His Heavenly love,
I feel His strength and love surround me
with awe and wonder from above.
He always is there to comfort me,
or walk with me in times of strife,
He is my Alpha and Omega
and gives me the purpose of my life.
In the hands of God, I can do all things
as He strengthens me to face the day.
In the hands of God, I can find peace,
and know He will always lead the way.
In the hands of God, I am His, forever.

The Hand of Christ

Christ extended His hand to Peter,
as he was swept into the raging sea,
and rescued him from the churning waters,
and He will do the same for you and me.
His hand reaches out to us, as we struggle with our sins,
we know He is there to redeem us,
but we sometimes just ignore
His helping hand of Grace and kindness,
when He is knocking at the door.
Christ's hand is there to bless us,
and bring comfort to our soul,
as we ask for His forgiveness,
and His strength to make us whole.
Christ's hand of compassion will guide us
to find our path on the road of life,
as we bless and reach out helping others
who are dealing with sorrow and strife,
we can become the hand of Christ.

In The Arms of Christ

In the arms of Christ, I can find forgiveness,
In the arms of Christ, I can find my way,
He consoles me in my sorrow,
and leads me through each precious day.
In the arms of Christ, I can find my healing,
and can find true peace and love,
as His loving arms enfold me,
I can trust in my Lord above.
I pray to Him for strength and Mercy,
as I face my sins, and those of the world each day,
I know His love and Grace surround me,
and that He will always show me the way.
I am so blessed He's with me now,
He is my Savior and my friend,
I can rest in His loving arms,
and know He will be with me forever,
to the end.

Spiritual Eyes, Spiritual Heart

What can we see with our Spiritual eyes
as they are focused on God
and His Mercy and Grace,
as He leads us His way,
where can we find our place,
and walk closely with Him?

What can we feel with our Spiritual heart,
when we trust in His Word,
and His compassion and love,
that brings joy and peace
as He guides us from above,
and we walk surrounded by Faith?

With our Spiritual eyes and Spiritual heart,
we can see and feel and rejoice,
in His wondrous creations,
His everlasting love and forgiveness,
and the hope of Eternal life.

III
Spiritual Light and the Cross

The Cross Points The Way

By the tender mercy of our God,
the dawn from on high will break upon us,
to give light to those who sit in darkness,
and in the shadow of death, to guide our feet,
into the way of peace.
Luke 1:78-79

God's Light

Surround yourself with God's Light,
let it encircle you and protect you
as you face challenges we must meet.
Look to Him on the Cross
and fall at His feet.
Let it bring comfort to your soul,
and heal the brokenness and wounds
to let you know all is well,
and again make you whole.
Though there may be negative
thoughts and words from some,
as you bravely step forward
you can look to The One
whose peace you will feel
and His Grace and Mercy so true,
they are always there,
and are forgiving and real.
As His Light shines in your heart,
His path you will see,
and know of His guidance
as He walks beside you and me.

He Is Still The Light

In our troubled and turbulent world,
when things somehow don't seem right,
as we face what each day brings,
we know whatever comes our way
that Jesus is still The Light.
When we struggle to understand
why our world is filled with hate,
and people kill and are angry and fight,
we can turn to Him in our sadness
and know that Jesus is still The Light.
He is there for us when we do wrong,
and gives us His Mercy and forgiving Love,
We can rest assured that He loves us
and that God's glory shines from above.
When we face loss, and we grieve,
He gives us strength so we can believe,
and can walk by faith and not by sight,
and even in the darkest night,
know deep in our hearts,
that Jesus is still The Light.

The Light of Christ

In our sometimes dark and uncertain world,
when it seems there is no light,
the light of Christ shines brightly,
as we walk by Faith and not by sight.
With God's power over darkness,
and His transforming love,
there is no absence of Spiritual light
and we praise His glory from above.
We can be like Christ's light in the world,
as we know His goodness and love,
and share God's Word with those who doubt,
and carry a heavy load,
searching for a way to lighten their burden,
as they travel down a very dark road.
God's Grace and Mercy will lead them
to find forgiveness and His love,
and the promise of Eternal life,
as the light of Christ shines from above.

Child of Darkness

Not seeing,
Not seeing Jesus.
No vision...no light...
Blindness...Darkness...
You are my Child...
Awareness.
Awakening,
Illumination,
Surrender...
Eyes opening,
Seeing,
Seeing life...
Seeing life shining
through Jesus Christ,
our Savior.

I Am Moving Towards Your Light

I am chosen by you, Jesus,
I am chosen by you.
I am moving towards your light
as it shines through the darkness,
and now I see, the price you paid for me.
I am chosen by you, Jesus,
I am chosen by you…
I feel your Spirit, your love touches me,
and now I see, how you saved me.
You came to give me life,
and paid the price on the Cross,
you saved me when I was forgotten, and lost.
I am chosen by you, Jesus,
I am chosen by you…
I am moving towards your light,
as it shines through the darkness,
I feel your Spirit,
and your love,
for me.

The Cross Points The Way

The message of the Cross,
touches me with His love, His suffering.
Jesus died for me to live,
and my sins He did forgive.
His healing power is there
as with Him I walk each day,
I find my strength to carry on,
as the Cross points the way.

Look for the Cross,
It points the way to His love.
Look for the Cross,
It points to our Lord above.
By His Grace I am saved,
He has set me free,
He died so I could live
and gave His salvation to me.
At the cross my sins are laid,
and, by Him, with love and Grace
I find true joy,
and am wondrously made.

Touched By The Cross

We are touched by the Cross,
as we come to pray,
you can feel the presence of Lord Jesus,
as the sun rises in the sky,
and think about His suffering,
and how He hung on the Cross to die.
You can contemplate His Mercy,
and His forgiving Love,
His amazing Grace we don't deserve,
and the glory that shines from above.

We are touched by the Cross,
as we bow our heads, and pray,
and praise Him as our Savior, Son of God,
Emmanuel, Christ the hope of glory.
On the Cross He died for our sins,
so we could have His Eternal Love and Mercy.
On that joyless day He was crucified,
and suffered in agony,
and now we can live with hope and see,
that we are now, and will forever be,
touched by the Cross for Eternity.

The Cross and the Crown

From the Cross to the Crown,
we search for meaning, understanding.
Jesus died for us on the Cross,
so we could follow Him, and have Eternal life.
With His Grace, we can receive
His Mercy and Love, and find the pathway
to forgiveness in our hearts and minds.
He is there to lift us to heaven,
to bring us closer to the glory of God,
where we can inherit
the Crown of Righteousness,
through the righteousness of Christ,
an everlasting crown,
for all who love the Lord,
and believe in His promises.
Though we encounter discouragements,
and at times persecution and suffering,
we know our reward is with Christ,
and we will find our peace, and rest,
with Him in Eternity,
as we are led from the Cross to the Crown.

IV
God's Wonders

Chickadee

Who is like you, O Lord, among the gods?
Who is like you, majestic in holiness,
awesome in splendor, doing wonders?
Exodus 15:11

Chickadee

Sweet Chickadee,
tiny winged wonder
of God's world,
sits still and silent,
observing Autumn colors
turning the surrounding landscape
into a forest of flame and gold.
He senses the changing season,
as the earth prepares for winter,
his world will be transformed
into a wintry scene,
of crisp, snowy days,
that he welcomes,
when he will sing
his song.

The Almighty Artist

At times I pause to think about
the many wonders of God surrounding us.
Azure skies, emerald trees, sunlit seas,
shimmering with God's own jewelry...
The flash of crimson feathers,
Spider webs with raindrops
trickling down their silken trails,
with beads of sparkling silver...
We are but minute images
within a world so amazing to behold.
If we look beyond the soiled streets,
the corruption of the cities,
the clashes of our cultures,
we become a part of the painting,
done on the canvas of nature,
by the Almighty Artist.
We are swept up in the swirl
of person, to person,
nation to nation,
and man to universe...
God holds the paintbrush,
but we form the colors
of the world.

Winter On The Horizon

Tall, dark trees,
stretch their limbs,
and reach upwards,
sensing a chill in the air.
Winter is on the horizon,
as Autumn lingers,
and God spreads a canopy
of her colors, across the sky,
and changing landscape.
He transforms the season,
from flame-colored leaves,
to frosty white imprints,
that the hills will embrace,
as Winter's snowy blanket
soon will cover the land.

Reflections On Our Wondrous God

God of sea and sky,
we marvel at your creations,
you call to us with visions,
that only you can provide.
Beneath the waves lie treasures,
but we cannot perceive their truth,
as it lives in the ebb and flow of the tide.
You give us magical moments,
that night and day we can embrace,
above us in starlit and sunset skies,
or the indescribable mysteries of space.
We try to live in your image, O God,
and anchor our trust in You,
You guide us in our daily lives,
giving wisdom and strength anew.
You are God of all life,
our Holy and Wondrous God,
we forever give our Praise,
and humble thanks to You.

Glory To God

Majesty...wonder...
The heavens declare His glory...
His Radiance bursts forth
in clouds of color...
His magnificent fingerprint
touches the sky, melting together
glorious shades of beauty,
with His Love, His Grace,
and our faith.

Majestic Wonder

Early golden rays of light
touch the land below,
reflecting God's presence
and strength.
Reaching skyward,
mountains embrace them
with their rising peaks
of openness and beauty,
in patterns of varied color.
As daylight fades,
deep shadows surround
the aura shining from above,
as it echoes God's majesty
and wonder.

Glorious Nature

Emerald waters
embrace the shoreline,
of trees and earth.
Gently sloping hills
reflect shadows
of brilliant light
shining from above.
Sunlit golden streams
cascade warmth
down upon earthen places.
The fullness of God's artistic touch,
open upon the landscape,
in endless wonder,
brings forth the glorious images
of Nature's beauty to life.

Diamonds of Joy

Diamonds of silver white,
descending from above,
falling gently.
God made…each design unique…
Fine streaks, barely seen,
then increasing in intensity.
Visions of white, sparkling, swirling,
one of the many wonders of God,
filling the landscape with layers,
transforming the earth
into an ivory white blanket.
Snowflakes now falling quickly,
surrounding me in beauty;
I breathe in the wonder of them,
as they touch my face,
and I taste their wet coldness
on my tongue.
I lift my head and look upward,
giving thanks to Him,
and laugh with joy…

Sometimes, when it seems like we are struggling in stormy seas in our lives, we search, and long for tranquility and peace, like this sea creature, seeking Divine direction. We have the reassurance that God will direct us as we navigate our way, and lead us in the direction we should go.

Seeking Divinity

Innocent sea creature of God,
makes his way through the crystal waters,
searching for tranquility and peace.
Splendor radiates above him,
encircling his head,
with virtue and vulnerability.
Slowly and gracefully
he navigates through
the sometimes stormy seas,
seeking Divine direction,
and a place where he
can be free.

Just as our planting of seeds yields new growth, so God wants our faith to grow and be nourished, to sustain us in our lives, so that we will reap an abundant harvest, and bear the Fruits of the Spirit, in the ways of joy, patience, love, kindness, gentleness, goodness, faithfulness, and self-control.

Seeds of Earth

Seeds of Earth,
sown to reap an abundant harvest,
of life…of sustenance.
Seeds of earth,
God's wonders in action,
captured by Nature's boundaries;
on the trees, fruit to ripen,
for the eye to see,
for our body to be sustained,
as in the Fruits of the Spirit.
Seeds of earth,
planted to grow, replenish,
and bring new life to the world.

Like stone fortresses, we need to stand strong for our Lord, and our faith. He is our strength, our solid foundation for our lives. God shows us the path to our destiny, and, just as they portray a positive presence of stability, He wants us to portray a positive presence of our Christianity in our lives.

Standing Strong

Standing strong,
with solid foundations,
Stone fortresses
exhibit their variations
of rugged quality.
With their unique beauty, and stature,
they portray a positive presence of stability,
that reinforces their destiny,
and God's place for them
in the world.

Roots are important to plants, trees, flowers, vegetables, and even weeds, but our roots are important to us, in our daily lives. God nurtures our roots, as we grow in our faith, and gives us His guidance and wisdom, as we grow in new life for Him.

Taking Root

Roots …one of God's wonders…
Far below the surface,
our roots take hold,
as we grow in our faith,
and trust in God.
We grow and change,
as He provides the foundation,
and nurtures our roots,
to give strength and purpose
to us, in our world…our lives…
Though invisible to the eye,
whether in nature, or faith,
roots remain the source
of strength and growth,
and new life, for all living things.

Early mornings are a perfect time to connect with God – to take time to pray and meditate on His Word, before our lives get busy, and the world demands our attention. It is a peaceful, restful time to reflect, listen to God, and thank Him for the many blessings He provides for us.

Misty Morning

Morning mist envelops the trees,
stretching their bare branches
as Winter holds them.
They look longingly toward Spring,
as a Rose-tinted sky offers shadows
on God's serene landscape.
In the distance, a hint of Spring beckons,
where life is starting anew
in minute green patches.
Traces of mist linger,
then peacefully ascend,
slowly drifting over the still water,
awaiting their time
to silently disappear
into the day.

Just a walk on the beach will bring us close to a multitude of God's imaginative and amazing creations that we can enjoy. His wonders yield many different treasures, and give us a glimpse of the magic of the seashore.

Seashore Magic

Magical seashore images
paint a palette of varied color;
they blend together beauty and strength
of God's amazing creations.
Perfect shells, and sand dollars,
reflect a kaleidoscope of colors,
and many different shapes,
as they merge with the aura of life on the beach.
Children digging in the sand,
shell hunters walking leisurely,
sunbathers drinking in the golden rays,
waders enjoying the tumbling clear waters,
where waves can magnify the glorious colors
of the beach treasures,
and beckon another beachcomber
to embrace God's seashore magic once again.

Sometimes it seems like our lives are like rushing rivers and churning seas – always in motion – sometimes turbulent…Our Lord wants us to stop, and take a deep breath and close our eyes and remember to "Be Still, and Know That I am God."…

Rushing

Streams in motion,
Descending,
Advancing…evolving,
Sliding…gliding,
Falling…flowing,
Rushing…

Churning

Swirls of colors,
cast a golden phosphorescent glow,
tumbling with turbulent intensity…
Clouds of froth and foam combine,
rising and falling
with the uncertain
and always changing sea,
constantly churning endlessly.

V
Our Christian Journey

Faraway Thoughts

Then He said to them all, "If any want to become my followers, let them deny themselves and take up their cross daily and follow me..."

Luke 9:23

Faraway Thoughts

Gazing out across an expanse of land,
bathed in God's light,
at times faraway thoughts can call to us
in our meditations and times of prayer.
Thoughts that God loves us, and cares,
and gives us a bridge
of kindness, hope and love,
so we may connect to others
and share our Christian faith.

As time moves on in our lives,
we can rest assured, He is there for us,
to listen, to guide and strengthen us,
and give us wisdom.
Our thoughts may seem to be faraway,
but we must remember,
our sovereign God is close to us,
and His blessings are endless.

I Will Follow Your Lead

I will follow your lead, my Lord,
to where you want me to go,
I know you are here by my side,
though the path may be steep and slow,
I know that I must go
wherever you lead me.

I will follow your lead, my Lord,
to where you want me to go,
to reach out to those who need to know
your amazing Grace and Love so true,
who you are, and what you can do,
I trust you, and will lean on you.
Every breath I take is your gift to me,
you forgave my sins at Calvary,
I give you all the glory,
and will become all I can be,
if I follow your lead.
I will follow your lead, my Lord, and know,
that you will send me
to where you want me to go.

Our Journey

Our life is a journey,
a journey of struggles and beliefs,
a journey of discovery,
as we search for Jesus,
and follow Him,
to find a place, a purpose, and peace
in our hearts, with His Grace.
Our life is a journey,
a journey of hope and faith,
a journey with Jesus,
as we follow Him,
to find a home, a passion, and praise
in our hearts, with His Love...
A journey of hope, a journey of faith,
we look up to Him,
and give God all the glory.
Our life is a journey,
and we follow Jesus,
to find a place, purpose, and peace
in our hearts, with Him, forevermore...

Jesus Is Our Hope

In our often confusing and stressful world,
we search for wisdom and strength;
in times of fear or sorrow,
when it is hard to cope,
we can pray and cry out to you, O Lord,
and, with faith, know there is hope.
Hope is found, as God reveals
His caring and His love,
for we are His children, and we are one,
we can depend and lean on Him,
when skies seem gray, and there is no sun.
We can come to Him in our despair,
and we have His reassurance,
He is our Rock and Salvation, and will be there,
to take us through the difficult times,
when we are lost, and need His care.
Whatever is troubling to our soul,
with faith, we can face the future,
knowing Jesus is our hope,
and He will make us whole.

A Tree of Life

The Ways of God are a tree of life,
His branches reach out to us
with love, mercy and forgiveness.
They are our grace in times of turmoil,
our shelter in sudden storms;
they give comfort and compassion
when we are lost and struggling,
and bring beauty in the changing seasons;
they deflect the falling raindrops and snow,
as they protect nature's young.
His tree stands mighty and strong,
against the evils of the world.
His Word is spoken throughout the forest
with murmurs of hope and faith.
As we honor Him with our Worship,
we must remember,
The Ways of God are a tree of life,
and of death, for our sins,
for our life eternal...for His Son, Jesus,
until we rise in glory to be with Him forever,
shining as the Sun.

Safe Harbor

Waves of Mercy, Lord,
for things that I have done,
Waves of Grace, from you, the Holy One,
surround me with your love,
be an anchor for me, as I sail the stormy sea,
and search for your Safe Harbor.
Waves of Mercy, Lord,
you know the things I've done
Waves of Grace, surround me Holy One,
give me your forgiveness,
be an anchor for me, as I sail the stormy sea,
and long for your Safe Harbor.
I sail through the stormy seas,
waves crash on the shore,
you guide my ship across them,
and know what I'm praying for.
Waves of Mercy Lord,
for things that I have done,
Waves of Grace, from you the Holy One,
surround me with your love,
be an anchor for me, as I sail the stormy sea,
and find your Safe Harbor.

Rising Higher

Rising higher,
You lead me through the storm,
though my wings are battered and worn,
you are beside me,
you will be beside me, forever.
Rising higher,
you guide me through the wind,
you take my hand and make me strong,
you are my strength,
you will be my strength, forever.
I'm rising higher, than ever before,
you have opened the door
so I can rise higher.
Rising higher,
you hold me close to you,
and keep me from harm,
you are my Savior,
you will be my Savior, forever.
I'm rising higher, than ever before,
you have opened the door
so I can rise higher...and higher.

When I Surrender

When I surrender, Lord,
I will offer my life to you,
your gift to me is all I am now,
and all that I hope to be.
When I surrender, Lord,
I will pray and worship you
as you fill me with your loving Grace,
and promise of eternity.
When I look up to the heavens,
and bow my head in prayer,
my heart will be full of your presence,
and I'll know you are always there.
When I surrender, Lord,
I will give my heart and life to you,
my gift to you is what I will become,
as I walk my journey of faith,
with hope to be someone,
forever in glory with you.
Jesus, you are the Light of my Life…

Lord, I am Yours

Surround me with your love, Lord,
cast my cares into the sea,
as I journey forth,
renew my faith, Lord, as I walk;
and, when I fall,
give me your hand, Lord,
and hold me close,
you forgave me,
and I am yours.

Surround me with your love, Lord,
I need your Grace and Mercy,
as I journey forth,
let me rise on Eagles wings
and soar above the storm.
As my earthly journey ends,
give me your hand, Lord,
and hold me close,
you died for me,
and I am yours,
for all eternity.

Christmas/Advent

For a child has been born for us
a Son given to us;
authority rests upon on His shoulders,
and he is named Wonderful Counselor,
Mighty God, Everlasting Father,
Prince of Peace
Isaiah 9:6

The Prince of Peace

"His Name Shall Be Called, The Prince of Peace"-Isaiah 9:6
He came into the world, as a precious baby,
with great presence, yet so small,
at the time no one understood
how his life would touch us all,
that we could receive His Forgiveness and Grace,
or that he would be the Prince of Peace.
He lay in the stable, so loving and mild,
the beloved one, Jesus, the Blessed Christ Child,
who would bring to all men, His Goodness and Peace,
and bring light to the world, so darkness would cease.
We rejoice, Joy to the World, we sing,
and think about the glorious time
when angels proclaimed the birth, of Christ, the King,
as they gathered above the stable in the night,
and therein was brought a wondrous sight,
as Jesus was born in Bethlehem,
to the joy of the shepherds and the three Wise Men.
He was the Indescribable Gift from God…Our Savior,
who died on the cross to give us His Peace here on earth,
and lives in our hearts, as we celebrate His birth,
"For unto us, a child is born, to us a son is given,
and He shall be called "The Prince of Peace".

Our Savior's Birth

O Come, O come, let us celebrate,
the birth of our dear Lord is here,
angels surround Him with heavenly radiance,
and tell of the Good News far and near,
they lift their voices to rejoice "It Came Upon the Midnight Clear".
Shepherds stand in awe and wonder,
as a star in the East shines brightly, this night,
they know this moment is different,
for they are surrounded by a heavenly light.
The Three Kings have come from a land afar,
and hear a cry echoing in the night,
and wonder why a star they followed so long
is so uncommonly bright.
They enter the stable, and fall to their knees,
and present their gifts in reverence,
of Gold and Myrrh and Frankincense,
for in the manger lies the baby Jesus,
so precious, with His love,
who will change the world, and bring glory to God above.
He is Immanuel, God with us, and will save us from our sins,
He will bring peace and joy on earth,
so let us celebrate and praise Him,
it is our Savior's birth...

Trust in the Lord, with all your heart
and do not rely on your own insight,
in all your ways acknowledge Him,
and He will make straight your paths...
Prov. 3:5.6

About the Author

Arla Olsen has been writing poetry since attending Middle School, in her hometown of Washington, D.C. She attended Colorado State Univ., in Ft. Collins, CO, concentrating her study on Journalism and Zoology. She has worked in the airline industry, in CA, and at a Mall Ministry in NJ. After moving to the Seattle area, she worked for the Boeing Co., and was honored by the Southcenter Seattle Chapter of the Business and Professional Women's Assn., as their Woman of the Year.

Arla, who writes under her pen name of Arla R. Jensen, has a collection of poems published entitled "Reflections of Life, of Love, of Loneliness", and a mystery adventure novel "Shadows on the Slopes". Her poetry has appeared in several publications, including "Portals", and also in poetry anthologies, "The Best of the Audubon Poets", "The Journey Continues", and "September 11."

As a member of East Woods Presbyterian Church, in Vancouver, WA, Arla serves as Elder of Adult Education, and leads the Women's Bible Study.

She is a nature lover, and has a deep fascination with owls and hot air balloons. She resides in Vancouver.

Printed in the United States
By Bookmasters